Sex-Terminating Angel

John Danen

Published by John Danen, 2023.

SEX-TERMINATING ANGEL

First edition. August 18, 2023.

Copyright © 2023 John Danen.

ISBN: 979-8224052776

Written by John Danen.

Table of Contents

Contact me. 1

Introduction. 2

The exterminating angel. 3

The sex-terminating angel. 4

Be above seduction. 7

The sex-terminating angel and men. 8

Final review of the levels and their consequences. 9

Level one. Teddy bears. 10

Level two. The fools. 11

Level 3. Semifools. 12

Level 4. The normal ones. 13

Level 5. The flirts. 14

Level 6. The seducers. 15

Level 7. The sexducers. 16

Level 8. The enslavers. 17

Level 9. The Dark Seducers. 18

Level 10. The sex-terminating Angels. 20

A bit of culture. 24

Seduction in the novel "Los gozos y las sombras". 26

Seduction in the novel "Fortunata and Jacinta". 30

Seduction in the novel "Cañas y barro". 35

The Great Reset. 39

Have a good time. 40

Production. 43

Release. 50

I am John Danen, the sexducer, the former angel sex-terminator... 52

Hypergamy. 56

The phoenix. 61

Hermes Gasparini. 62

Tricked game. 64

Be cheerful and fun. 65

The last men seducing at the end of days, once again. 67

The push and pull and the happy state. 69

The "yes" and the "noes". 73

Final advice. 76

Contact me.

If you want to ask me questions, ask me questions, or receive advice on seduction, I offer this service of seduction coach. I also offer courses. You can contact me through these links.

Links:

John Danen seduction - [1]YouTube

TikTok by johndanen (@johndanen) | Watch johndanen['2]s latest videos on [3]TikTok

John Danen seduction | [4]Facebook

John Danen seduction (@dark_seduction) - [5]Instagram photos and videos. [6]

---

1. https://www.youtube.com/channel/UCUOsfiulxHrzWkdjkx6scJg

2. https://www.tiktok.com/@johndanen

3. https://www.tiktok.com/@johndanen

4. https://www.facebook.com/0Dark000000

5. https://www.instagram.com/dark_seduccion/

6. https://www.instagram.com/dark_seduccion/

Introduction.

This is not going to be a book to teach seduction either, all that has already been left behind. This book is the book where good and evil meet. In this book I will tell you what a sex-terminating angel is and what his motivations are. I will also tell you about the difficulties of flirting with girls of higher social class, the joy and fun, I will decode novels and characters and explain them from the perspective of the seducer, I will talk about what is the production. Many things that complement what was written in the previous ones and give you more knowledge to fight and win in the game of love.

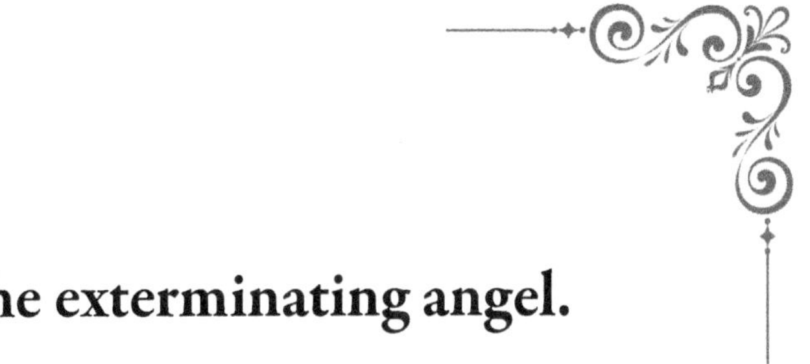

The exterminating angel.

I have been quite intrigued by the exterminating angels. Angels like Gabriel have appeared in movies, who enters a bar beating his head while sounding apocalyptic trumpets, and the truth is that I find it a fascinating subject. This angel has more power than any demon and although his acts are of great savagery, he fulfills the divine will, which sometimes is to exterminate an entire people, or the entire human race.

On the one hand he is a being of peace and love, and on the other a genocidal exterminator. The exterminating angel shows no mercy to the wicked.

The exterminating angel is an envoy of God who imparts justice, gives the kingdom of heaven to the good and exterminates sinners with a sword of fire.

This figure has inspired me a lot and I want to make it the central axis of this book. We have to be that, exterminating angels who give heaven or hell as they deserve it.

The exterminating angel is a being of light, who with wisdom, gives what he needs to each person with whom he interacts.

The sex-terminating angel.

The sex-terminating angel is a just man. He is the one who wants to do good, the one who is tired of suffering and making people suffer. He is a man tired of being normal, he is a man tired of being trampled on. He is also tired of being trampled on and of being bad. He is someone who wants this world to be better. To that end he rewards good and punishes evil. He is the one who stands up to balance things out. Someone with a lot of power and experience who has lived through everything and wants to help others. He is a man who wants to live and enjoy. He is a magnificent person who gives joy and happiness to everyone, and only in case he senses the intended abuse he will punish, that's why we say he is an angel. He has two faces: the good and funny positive face, and the dark face, the face of dark seduction.

Yes, we are angels because we do justice, we are sex because we do sex and terminators because many times we end up only in sex. We make sex and we finish, we finish with the relationship, but that is only a possibility, the normal thing is to continue, we can also finish with her self-esteem if we do evil in excess and really fuck the life of a good woman, that's why we measure our actions trying to avoid evil.

We do not cheat, nor do we hurt people for pleasure, but we are fair, we tell the truth, we say that we are flirts, that we are fuckers, that we want to have fun, that they do not fall in love with us, that we do not want to hurt or be hurt. Only if they are real bitches with us, we are going to apply the dark arts, which we also know how to do.

If we have to lie to achieve our objectives, we lie, but we lie very little, just enough, or we lie for a short period of time, and always with the objective of avoiding the suffering of others.

We know that a woman who falls in love with us is not convenient, because a chain of falling in love occurs. The men who go after her are also harmed. We are angels and we want to do good, and we try to do it, we are also sex-terminators and if some is bad with us we can really exterminate her with our tremendous power.

The exterminating angel goes on the march, he is kind but not foolish, he camouflages his wisdom, he metamorphoses to be valid for the girl, he deceives but very little and avoids evil. He has great power and uses it to seduce and also not to harm, he does not want to harm.

When a bad woman has deliberately done us a lot of harm, deceived us, used us, screwed us and done everything that we avoid doing with her when we could easily do it, then and only then do we use dark seduction, in the necessary dosage to screw her too, because it is also our mission to exterminate bad people from this game.

Always thinking about the consequences of what we do and whether it will be beneficial for her or detrimental. Many times it is harmful for her to go around fucking men, abusing them and leaving them in a fucking mess with her lies and falsehoods; that is why we cut this circle of pain, because behind those men fucked by her are women who are also fucked by these men, because they do not pay attention to them and therefore they suffer as well. So we reestablish the balance and stop the **chain of pain** by doing evil.

We have to do it only when it is strictly necessary, we usually create **a chain of good,** not letting this woman fall in love with us. So we leave her fit to go with others, so everyone will have their share of the cake. We do not want to hoard too much, only to hoard what is necessary, which we already hoard a lot, we let the others have their chance.

If we were total bastards we would fall in love and make many women suffer, and there would be this chain of pain. But we don't want that, we want us to be their joy. We give joy but we are also someone that they know will not reciprocate, and many of them will at least fall out of love and will be able to go out to the game, and thanks to that other nice guys will enjoy them too.

The angel is above getting too many or too few, he has already gotten a lot of women and he does what he has to do. Restore the balance, he will take only what is necessary, so that all men and women benefit from their interaction.

I am the **sex-terminating Angel**, the destroyer, the scourge of evil, the being of light and the Dark seducer, the one who balances the system.

Be above seduction.

When you have done everything, achieved all your goals, punished, forgiven, been good and been bad, in the end the mission you have is to contribute your enormous experience for the benefit of others. You are a being of light that brings joy and happiness. Through the practice of seduction you transcend seduction itself and become a kind of heavenly envoy who gives them what they need. If she has been placed at your side, it is because she has been chosen from above and you must fulfill your mission.

What girl is she? What does she need? What can you bring to her? Yes, you have to be kind, because life already punishes by itself, your punishing function will only be required on rare occasions in which you are the executing angel that guides the sword of fire, but normally it is not necessary to fulfill this function. So after decades and decades you no longer dedicate yourself to seduce because you already do that automatically without paying attention to it, what you dedicate yourself to is, to evaluate if that girl is worthy of the gifts you could give her, and if she is, to think about what she needs that you can give her. You also think at the level of society in general, if what you do is good or bad for the whole. It's usually good to prey, to make your production, to make his suitors hopeless, to impose your tyranny. That's what's best for you and for the whole.

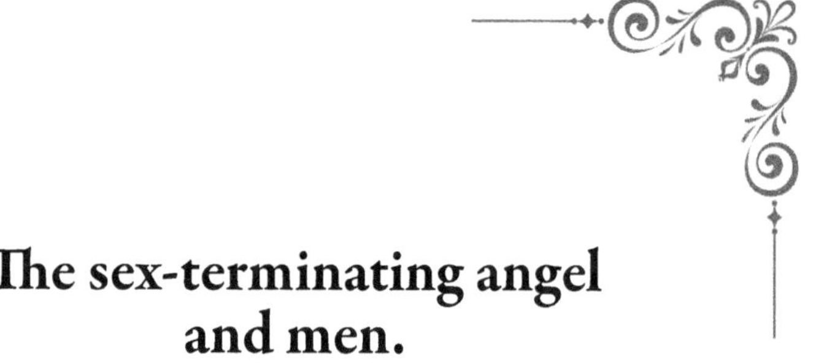

The sex-terminating angel
and men.

Men who try to compete with you must learn the lessons, you are their teacher, a supreme teacher who gives them the terrible punishment for their ineptitude. The men are taught by you, you do good. You take them out of the game, let them find another! You hoard. You show the way, you bring them back to the harsh reality. You exterminate them.

You don't just seduce the one you don't care about, you overwhelm, massacre and exterminate all the unskilled who cross you. You don't do it because you are evil, on the contrary, you are kind and give them what they deserve, extermination. Either they learn the way or they must succumb. You are someone who helps them see things clearly, they should be grateful that you execute them. Some will get over it and get better. You clear the playing field. You love them because you were once like that in your early days, so you annihilate them. They need to be annihilated for them to get better. You create the pain, but you **break the circle of pain**. You harden them, women will see them as more attractive after your input. And so by hoarding, overwhelming, being irreverent, defiant, boastful and ruthless, you do great good under the guise of great evil.

Final review of the levels
and their consequences.

The key to understand what is a sex-terminator angel is in the levels, so by analyzing each one we will understand how to reach this level ten. The level of the sex-terminator angel.

Level one. Teddy bears.

Teddy bears are the lowest level there is. They are the typical friend who is in the friendzone forever. They listen to all their stuff, they comfort. They see them as men without dicks, as asexual beings and will never have anything loving or sexual with them.

They do. Good, they do good clearly, an **infinite good** that gives peace and unconditional love.

They receive. Evil, the most absolute evil. They are paid with **enormous sadism** for the great good they did. They are **punished to death**.

They do. They do evil with them, **a terrible and sadistic evil**. And they don't even feel bad.

They receive. They are empowered to the fullest, they **value themselves as goddesses** because of all the adulation they receive.

Society. Society is **infinitely harmed** by the actions of these teddy bears, because they end up **committing suicide or in psychiatric hospitals**. What they do is to **raise enormously** the market price, they raise a lot the requirements that women put, because they are super valued and therefore they are going to restrict their access. This will cause **difficulty** to be able to flirt with other men, because sometimes they want that all of them fulfill the ridiculous requirements that these flatterers do fulfill.

Level two. The fools.

Fools fall in love, fools are soft, fools live on illusions. One of the most important characteristics of fools is that they tell everyone about their love projects. Projects that never come to fruition. They make fools of themselves by giving the image of desperate people to their friends.

They do. Good, they do good, clearly an **enormous good** that gives peace and unconditional love. A good only slightly less great than the previous ones.

They receive. Evil, they are paid with **sadism** and punished **harshly**.

They do. They do evil with them, a **terrible and sadistic** evil. They care the same as the others, nothingness.

They receive. They are empowered almost to the maximum, they **value themselves as superior** because of all the adulation they receive.

Society. Society is **greatly harmed** by the actions of these fools, because they end up with **very serious mental problems** and raising the market price a lot. The requirements placed on women are **much** greater than before, they are much more valued and therefore will restrict their access, this will cause difficulty to be able to flirt with other men.

Level 3. Semifools.

Half-wits are the smart friends of fools, they differ from them because despite coming from the world of fools, they are more successful with women because they are less soft and are a little better at seducing.

They do. Good, they do good clearly, a very great good. A good only **a little less great** than the previous ones.

They receive. Evil, they are paid back **quite sadistically** and **punished harshly**.

They do. They do evil with them, **quite terrible and sadistic** evil. They care very little about them

They receive. They become very empowered, they value themselves as **superior** because of all the adulation they receive.

Society. Society is **seriously harmed** by the actions of these half-wits, as they end up with **serious mental problems** and raise the market price **quite a lot**. The requirements placed on women are **greater** than before, they are **much more valued** and therefore will restrict their access, this will cause difficulty to be able to flirt with other men. The difficulty that the first three groups cause for others to pick up other men is similar, because women realize that they cannot demand from normal people the crazy things that they do for them.

Level 4. The normal ones.

Normal people are just that, normal, neither smart nor stupid. They have had a few affairs and girlfriends in their youth and have married sooner rather than later. They are quiet, or semi-quiet in their marriage.

They do. Good, they do good, a great good. A good only **a little less great** than that of the previous ones.

They receive. Evil, they are repaid with **some sadism** and **punished quite a bit**.

They do. They do evil with them, a **moderate** evil. They care little for them.

They receive. They are very empowered, they value themselves **much higher** because of the high valuation they receive.

Society. Society is **quite damaged** by the performance of these normal men, because they end up with **mental problems** and raising the market price **a little**. The requirements placed on women are **somewhat higher** than before, they are **more valued** and therefore will restrict their access, this will cause difficulty to be able to flirt with other men.

Level 5. The flirts.

The flirts are guys who are very spry and manage to seduce quite a few girls and who have their good times, especially in their youth. Some of them take a while to get married and that's why they do a little bit of trolling. They are less soft, their problem is that they do not maintain their dedication over time.

They do. Good, they do good, a moderate good. A good that rarely turns to evil.

They receive. Evil, they are repaid with **usury** and **punished a little**.

They do. They do evil with them, a **small** evil. They only care a little about them.

They receive. They are empowered, they value themselves **higher** because of the valuation they receive.

Society. Society is somewhat **harmed** by the performance of these flirts, because they could end up with **mental problems** and raising the market price. The requirements placed on women are **the same** as before, they are **just as valued as before** and therefore they will not restrict their access, this will not cause other men to worsen the difficulty in being able to flirt.

Level 6. The seducers.

Seducers are clearly already a high level. They are guys who are dedicated to seduction and who perceive themselves as different from the rest. Their career perseveres and although they have downturns due to engagements, even marriages, they resurface and reappear in the market, a place where they are more comfortable. They are high-level seducers, but not very high.

They do. Good and evil, they do little good, and sometimes little evil.

They receive. Evil, they are paid **little** and **punished occasionally** if they slacken in wickedness.

They do. They do evil with them, an **occasional** evil. They care a lot if they do evil and little if they do good.

They receive. They stay as they were, they are valued **the same as before** and sometimes their value is lowered.

Society. Society remains unchanged by the performance of these seducers, they finish well and the market price remains stable. The requirements placed on women are slightly **lower** than before, they are **just as valued as before with a downward trend,** and therefore will facilitate their access, this will cause other men some ease to be able to flirt.

Level 7. The sexducers.

Sexeducers combine seduction with sex and a lot of girls who pick up girls, fuck them. They are very sexual. They perceive themselves as the ultimate, the predator, the Alpha male. They are aware of the enormous power they have, which is far superior to everyone else. They have a resume that is more than 10 times that of a normal guy, being able to get hundreds of chicks hooked up and in some extreme cases hundreds of chicks fucked as well.

They do. Evil, they do little evil and sometimes very little good.

They receive. Good, they are paid **a lot** and **rewarded a lot** if they squeeze in evil.

They do. They do good with them, a **frequent** good. They care a lot if they do bad and a lot if they do good.

They receive. They lower their value, they are valued **less than before** and sometimes much less.

Society. Society benefits from the performance of these sex workers, they end up great and the market price sometimes drops a lot. The requirements placed on women are **much lower** than before, they are **less valued than before with a tendency to a big drop** and therefore will facilitate their access, this will cause other men much easier to pick them up. They will feel less important, more humble, they will become nicer. In the end they will be touched and then others will be able to be with them, although they themselves know that the following ones will not be at the height of the sex-producers and they will feel a little sad for this.

Level 8. The enslavers.

S lavers pick up girls with their sex-driving power, bring them into the world of sadomaso and make them their sex slaves.

They do. Evil, they do great evil and sometimes small evil.

They receive. The good, they are paid **a great deal** and **rewarded enormously**.

They do. They do good with them, a **regular and very great** good. They care a lot about them.

They receive. Their value drops enormously, they are valued **much less than before** and sometimes they are valued very little and the enslaver does with them almost whatever he wants.

Society. Society is greatly benefited by the performance of the enslavers, they end up great and the market price is greatly reduced. The requirements placed on women are **much lower** than before, they are much **less valued than before with a tendency to humility,** and therefore will greatly facilitate their access, this will make it much easier for other men to pick them up. They will feel much less important, more humble, they will become much nicer. In the end they will be very touched and then others will be able to be with them, although they themselves will know that the following ones will not be at the height of the enslavers and they will feel very sad for this.

Level 9. The Dark Seducers.

The Dark seducers seduce girls around with their power, get them into the world of sadomaso, make them sex slaves and punish them harshly for any abuse that any girl performs. They punish physically with sadomasochism and mentally with Dark actions. They try to avoid evil because they are aware of their power, but if any girl, because of her bad behavior, deserves the dark actions, here the Dark will be at ease punishing and enjoying the punishment he gives.

They do. Absolute evil, they do immense evil and sometimes enormous evil.

They receive. The good, they are paid **enormously** and **rewarded at the highest level**.

They do. They do good with them, **enormous** good. They care so much about them. They suffer sometimes terribly.

They receive. They lower their value to the maximum, they are valued **much less than before** and quite often they are not valued at all and are toys in the hands of the Dark seducer.

Society. Society is super benefited by the performance of the Dark seducers, they end up great and the market price is lowered a lot. They rebalance the market. The requirements placed on women are **much lower** than before, they are much **less valued than before with a tendency to kindness** and therefore will facilitate their access, this will make it much easier for other men to pick them up. They will feel much less important, more humble, some will even become good. In the end they will be very touched, and then others will be able to be with them, but they themselves will know that the following ones will not be at the height of the Dark seducer, and they will feel very sad about this until they get over it with time. If they do.

Level 10. The sex-terminating Angels.

The sex-terminator angels are people who have already done everything, who have already fulfilled everything, who have already been everything before, who are tired of doing evil, and after doing so much evil, they are good again. They have gone full circle, they have died, they have been reborn, they have gone through crises in which it seemed that their life of seducers was totally over, and they have come back to live again. To live another life when they thought it was all over. They are like the phoenix that rises from the ashes. In the past they were soft, stupid, clever, cleverer, cleverer, bastards, more bastards, bad, very bad, enslavers, they made their massacres, their monstrous productions, their dark actions, they gave their terrible punishments. All this they did in several cycles, they retired, but they came back again to the game.

They are people who are above good and evil, who should no longer have to be here, people whose time should have ended decades ago, but there they are totally contravening all the rules of the market by their enormous power. They become immortal in seduction, and cannot be wiped off the seduction map by extreme age or anything else.

They return to the game again but watching it from above, watching how all the poor people enjoy themselves and suffer. It is as if they were already dead and watching everyone doing what they have been doing for so long. But they are alive and still playing. They play very hard.

But they no longer want to be good and they no longer want to be bad, now they want to be fair and benefit society in general with their participation. They also want to help others to bond and reach their almost divine level.

The sex-terminating Angels have no great drive to achieve big wins, no big numbers, no big mischief, they just enjoy playing and are freed from chasing records and making the big sacrifices it all requires.

This complacency does not produce better results than in the previous levels, because they are really engaged only when they feel like it and do what they feel like doing, above good and evil.

Really **the maximum level is the Sexducer**. At that level you are concerned with production, you want to produce, mass produce, make a massacre. From that level on, which is the maximum level, you start to go crazy and you go up a level at the cost of doing some pretty crazy things.

Thus the enslaver stops caring so much about production and begins to care more about **enslaving production**, since he already has a huge number of women he has conquered and is looking for new things.

The Dark seducer, knowing all his power and his ability to make them submissive to the master, to enslave them physically and mentally, wants to rise as a vigilante and instead of dedicating himself to mass production as the sex producer, he dedicates himself to flirting, but **with a tendency to look for bad women to** punish and apply his sadism, with which he also goes quite crazy. He thinks he is the one who balances the system, the one who by doing evil does good and he is right, but also because of these airs of grandeur his production goes down.

Even more so, the sex-terminating angel who believes that he is above all and so he is, and who no longer worries about producing or punishing excessively, only about being in the game, goes out of his mind.

This is what can happen to you if you keep on seducing en masse, that there will come a day when you will go out of your mind and become a slaver, or Dark seducer, or sex-terminating angel.

What I am telling you will happen at least from the age of 40 and maybe from the age of 50 with more probability. Actually, if you want to increase your legend in terms of numbers, you should never go higher than level seven, sexductor level, because all these higher levels are a bit crazy. They will give you more power, yes, a power of mastery, a qualitative power, but not quantitative. Your resume, your production, will be quite a bit less. So I recommend that you never go higher than the sexducer level, so you'll really add up to the highest numbers.

I believe that you can't stay indefinitely in sexductor because it is very tiring. That's why the natural thing is that you realize that you have already done so many numbers that you feel like doing other things, you feel like enslaving, you feel like punishing, or that you think you are the sex-terminating angel, the one who is above everything and everyone, and that you don't even worry about winning, nor about overwhelming, but about simply being there like God judging everyone else and exterminating useless people in the process.

So even if you have reached level ten, which I have reached, I recommend restarting by dropping three levels and becoming a simple sex producer again. A hard-working and dedicated sexducer who strives to make his production, forgetting about the following levels that only slow down the production and make you go too far out of your mind. So to become powerful again, you have to go down a level, stay at sexducer and not go up from there.

And so going around the circle you lower the level and restart again motivated, again with illusion in adding up, with illusion in making massacres, with illusion in making big amounts again and that is where you should be. As long as you are in life you are in the struggle. You have to be as productive as possible, produce and produce until you can't do it anymore. Then again you go up a level to rest a little bit, and you punish, you enslave, or you are a sex-terminating angel, you rest a little bit at those levels and you go back again and again to mass production, and you keep it up as long as you can. And so dying and being reborn several times, you go on your way to death happy and carefree.

I myself renounce being a sex-terminating Angel and consider myself a sexducer again. I've already done so many things that I want to be one more. And this is the story of how one becomes a sex-terminating angel and how one renounces it.

They do. The good.

They receive. The good because it is such a high level that not even doing good can punish them, besides we don't care.

They do. They do good, and it almost doesn't matter what they do.

They receive. They receive good again.

Society. It benefits because there is movement. The sex-terminating Angel makes sex and abandons, not caring anything about love, nor about sex in excess, nor about production, nor about punishing. The angel sees to it that she does not come out harmed and abandons soon. She has sex and finishes. Hence the name sex-terminator. Sex terminator but without rage or revenge. He leaves them so that they do not suffer by falling in love with a real immortal vampire, who wants to be good, but knows how bad he is. In order not to harm them too much and to make them fall in love, you leave them early. Other times you don't give a shit about anything and sometimes you don't even leave a girl you are good with. You deepen sex and enjoy life.

The sex-terminating Angel is both angel and demon. He wants to empower the divine part. It is a dark seducer tired of evil.

Occasionally the angel lowers his divine level a bit and punishes as a Dark seducer, but only if he sees that it is good for society in general. This does not please the Angel, but he will do it if he has to.

In the end the Angel gets tired of being so nice and quiet and chooses to reincarnate again as a sexducer.

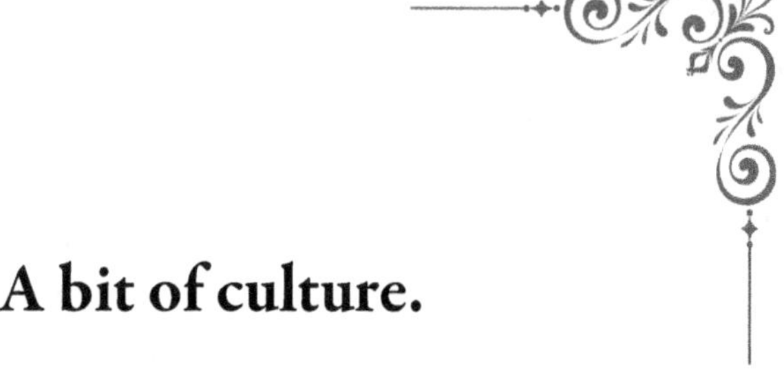

A bit of culture.

I can't help but be ecstatic when I see something perfect, solid, timeless, beautiful. That something I am referring to can be many things, a building, a statue, a book. It is time to stop being stupid as the Mexicans say, it is time to acquire a little culture in order to better understand seduction and life.

It is not enough to know how to seduce, that's for beginners, you have to know how to deal with girls once you've made a connection, you have to know about life. For this I look at the ancient writers who knew about life. In their works, sometimes hundreds of years ago, they already included very well reflected the seducers. Let's learn from these fictional characters, because they are not really fictional, they are modeled by their author imitating one or several real seducers he knew. People can invent almost nothing, no one can write about what they don't know, people reflect their world and their life. And if there are seducers in the novels it is because the author either is, or knows them perfectly well. Everything comes from his life experience, from observing people and understanding their behavior. Some of the seducers included in the books are so well reflected that I have no doubt that the author knew perfectly all the rules of seduction, that he knew everything and wanted to prove it by creating these characters. Now, centuries later, an equal recognizes his equal and values his work.

Thus, centuries before coaches and schools of seduction, there were writers who showed seduction in all its magnitude, the kind seduction and also the hardest, the Dark seduction.

I can attest that these seducers are excellent and that it is true that this is how we behave as it appears in novels. We think we know everything and that we are the best and the best, but in any past time there were always flirts, fuckers, and great masters, men who disguised under the guise of men according to the time, were great connoisseurs of life and seduction. So I am going to comment on several novels that I have read lately and I am going to translate them into the language of seduction. These novels are decoded and interpreted by my head to extract their essence so that you can, if you want to, read them and understand everything perfectly.

These novels have been encoded by a seducer, and can only be decoded and perfectly understood by another seducer.

The masters of space-time speak to us through these novels and it is necessary to know how to see beyond the appearance and the many accessory things that appear in them. In their essence they have teachings and show us what the reality of things is. A reality that is as **immutable** now as it was a century or two ago. It is necessary to think about the moment of space-time in which they were written and to understand that things could not be said openly as they are said now, but that they had to disguise the teaching with correct behavior, gallantry, and good manners. The teaching is there hidden behind many, many layers of cheesiness and ridiculousness of the time. These are things that you should not look at and that are there to hide the truth, things that had to be put on in order to be accepted by the masses and that were also put on because it was the way of feeling and expressing oneself at that time.

If they lived in the 21st century, they would be just like us.

Seduction in the novel
"Los gozos y las sombras".

There have always been two types of men in love, the winners and the losers. This has been reflected in novels and also in movies. This has always happened, the more beauty and the more wealth, the more and better women were obtained, especially in the past in which women were totally at the mercy of men, and had to marry whoever was a good match, that is to say, whoever could support them. Even if they did not like him, even if there were others more handsome and attractive, property, social position and wealth were the most important and decisive factor for them. This is reflected in Torrente Ballester's novel "Los gozos y las sombras",

This novel is set in Galicia in the 1930s. Don Cayetano, the town boss, does and undoes as he pleases and enjoys all the women in town, even the wives of his friends in the cantina. This man boasted of sleeping with all the beautiful girls in town and no one could take any of them away from him. In "Los gozos y las sombras" you can see that in this era of the 1930s, in pre-Franco Spain, there were very clear winners and losers. Ninety-nine percent were losers who were satisfied with having a woman, any woman, or rather the one they could afford to keep with their level of income.

When one has all the money and gives work to the whole town, all the women are indebted to him, because he places their husbands and gives them work. If this man wants to stop by any house to collect in kind the favor of having that family working, well, he goes and collects it, no one disputes anything. This, which is a novel, was very much like that in reality.

Only when a character from the aristocracy arrives, not so rich, but with status, wealthy relatives, possessions and influence, does Don Cayetano find a rival to match him in matters of seduction. These two men divide up the whole town in various ways.

Don Carlos, the new one, from education, modesty and respect in a certain way to women, a very strange respect that the only thing he does is to disguise as education his deep rejection to each one of them, who are totally ignored and tortured with his total indifference. Many of the women of the town make advances or tell him they like him, but he remains as cold as an iceberg, disguising his total aversion to them as correctness and good manners. He rejects all of them except one. It is precisely "La galana", Don Cayetano's most important lover, whom Don Carlos likes to seduce and seduces by rejecting all the others. Don Carlos is saying loudly with this, the only one I want is the one you value the most and I go and take her away from you. This causes a confrontation between the two, one from the gallantry and the most ancestral arrogance Don Cayetano, and the other Don Carlos a man with a lot of verbiage, who neither says yes nor no and misrepresents, manipulates and cajoles with his polite words that in the end say nothing.

My theory is that this Don Carlos is a misogynist to the maximum, since he rejects all the very good women that are offered to him in the town, and just to make him an ugly man and place himself above his rival Don Cayetano, he seduces the only one he could not flirt with, "la galana", who was Don Cayetano's official mistress.

A wonderful woman named Clara, with a somewhat licentious life but a very noble heart, is totally devoted to Don Carlos, he makes her suffer and suffer and tortures her with his total indifference. It is only when Cayetano notices her that Don Carlos claims her for his own.

Another woman of the highest social class who arrived in town was totally despised by Don Carlos, who pretended to be ignorant in order to displease her and get her to leave him alone. Deep down Don Carlos was looking for freedom, not to be tied to any woman, as he says several times in the novel that he prefers his freedom, both to live by himself and not to depend on anyone working for others, and not to depend on any woman, because he came precisely fleeing from a woman from Vienna.

I recommend that you read this novel because it will teach you many things, especially important is the character of Don Cayetano that I like very much and that although they put him as the bad guy of the novel, for me he enjoys my total sympathy, because deep down he is good, he doesn't lie to women, he doesn't lie to men, he goes around bragging about fucking everyone, and he is cheerful and partying, generous with his friends, and also with his friends' wives, whom he fucks and then calls their husbands cuckolded to their faces. This man is the shameless and brazen seducer who has no regard for anyone, whether they are deputies, mayors, bishops or whoever. They all pay obeisance to him, he is the fucking master of the city, he goes straight to the point and is direct.

While the main protagonist Don Carlos is a cunning man, cold, a misogynist, a man who hates women deeply and from education and gallantry despises them deeply, because none is at his level. He deceives everyone with his pretty words that say nothing. His great lover, the woman he is totally devoted to, Clara, suffers years and years of rejection, scorn and oblivion. He gives his love, or rather his fornication, to a brute peasant girl, to whom he also drags his feet and finally discards her, leaving her to marry another villager.

It is curious that between these two men there is the problem of deciding which one is more of a bastard. I think that this Don Carlos, whom everyone considers good, is much more of a bastard, because he makes women suffer a lot, playing the fool, playing the friend, the educated, the good man. But in his heart he feels totally above them all and he must consider them unworthy of belonging to his distinguished family. Therefore, just to satisfy his base instincts and to annoy the other, he seduces "the gallant". This man is cold, cunning, manipulative, he plays the good guy, but I don't like him very much. So hard and so cold for me he becomes a lost fool, because he loses countless opportunities. We can only understand what he does if we apply my theory that he is a deranged misogynist, who knows that the only way to really annoy women is to reject them all. A mgtow of antiquity.

While the other one gives them money, invites them, takes them around, makes them laugh, they all have their chance, he is a cheerful party animal and enjoyer, obviously Don Cayetano is the Sexductor, while the other one is a guy who disguised as goodness, he is ambiguous, he is not defined by one side or the other and he is really bad. So here the main protagonist is the bad guy, and the villain, at least from my point of view, is the good guy.

In the end they try to overthrow Don Cayetano and he defends himself against everyone, defeats all his enemies with a clean fist and they can not even among all the leaders of the people to finish him off.

I think this man Torrente Ballester who wrote this book was a very intelligent man. The author **divided what is a total seducer in two different men**. On the one hand we have the coldness of Don Carlos, who under the appearance of kindness is an absolute bastard. A man who to get to be so ruthless loses countless opportunities and does not enjoy anything to women, only enjoys his revenge which is to see them suffer for him, and the other Don Cayetano, on the contrary, is the charming scoundrel, the Sexductor who has a good time and enjoys with them.

To be really successful you have to be 75% Don Cayetano, the cheerful and partying fucker, and 25% Don Carlos, the bastard who enjoys watching them suffer more than enjoying them.

In the end they are both the same man in two different bodies, this novel is about me.

Seduction in the novel
"Fortunata and Jacinta".

This novel set at the end of the nineteenth century in Madrid, tells the adventures of two women, Jacinta, an upper class and good looking woman, who by social position is destined to marry a rich and handsome man; and Fortunata, a very low class woman who has to accept the company of any man who appears to her, and who lives calamities and misfortunes because of her social status. Fortunata is as beautiful or perhaps a little more beautiful than Jacinta, and she falls in love with our gallant Juan Cruz. With her he has a son who later dies. After these adventures he abandons her and is forced to marry Jacinta. But he cannot forget her and as soon as he finds out that she is back in the city he returns to look for her. Fortunata goes through many hardships and has to be admitted to a convent because there she will receive the education required by her new boyfriend, Maximiliano, a weak and sickly man who is not even a tenth of the man that Juan Cruz is and with whom she is forced to marry in order to survive. As soon as she leaves the convent, Juan Cruz is waiting for her and she does not take a day to return to him, deceiving her new husband, who was not even able to consummate the act on their wedding night, as he was ill.

Soon rumors of Fortunata's infidelities spread and the new husband, who I can't remember his name because of how stupid he is, ah yes, Maximiliano, goes to try to attack him and is so badly beaten that he almost dies.

In this novel we see a clear differentiation between the handsome seducer and the foolish pleaser in a very exaggerated way. One is a handsome handsome that I doubt that there was any man like that in Spain at that time, with that plant and that to my way of behaving so elegant and educated, a total gallant. The other was a fool in love, a very soft, very soft man who did nothing but cry, being sick and declaring his love for Fortunata, a little man who weighs barely 50 kilos. This little man, because of his social position, agrees to this woman who has to accept him because if he doesn't, he'll be out on the fucking street. Too much woman for him. Getting this woman against nature, simply for the money and position, is paid with constant infidelities, and a miserable life of cuckold.

Fortunata who is the protagonist of this novel returns again and again with her beloved Juan Cruz who again and again ends up getting tired of her and leaving her. She undergoes many sufferings and as soon as he appears again she goes back to him.

She leaves her husband and gets lost, but an older man takes advantage of the situation and makes her his mistress. She lets him do it because of her poverty and because the man is good without being stupid, he is a man who is just older. This man enjoys her but her health is already suffering from so much fucking and recommends her to go back to her husband. She goes back, but it is more of the same, the husband is a totally apocado man who does not offer any attraction for her, as soon as Juan appears she falls into the clutches of the seducer. But once again he leaves her again.

The poor woman goes through hardships, until she finally gets fed up with everything, she makes herself respected and says openly to everyone that she does not love her husband and that she loves the seducer, so she leaves her husband again and it seems that she finally joins her eternal love Juan Cruz. Fortunata gave birth to a child of Juan alone, even establishes contact with Jacinta's relatives, this Jacinta, Juan Cruz's wife, could not have children and wanted them very much. Many more things happen and finally this poor unfortunate woman dies and donates the child to Jacinta, but not without a fight with another lover of Juan, which is what finally cost her her life. Fortunata's husband, when he learns of her death, goes to the asylum headlong.

What lesson do we draw from all this? Well, a very hard lesson. That seducers suffer a little, that is, they suffer, but they recover easily because they have other lovers, deep down they love very superficially, but the damage they cause is tremendous. In Fortunata the damage is enormous because this woman always loves him and cannot forget him, and she literally dies for him fighting with another woman who has also been his lover. Jacinta, his wife, suffers a lot, and in the end everyone suffers a lot. The one who suffers the least is the one who makes everyone suffer, Juan Cruz, the seducer, the one who does tremendous damage. And here comes the important question

Love is perpendicular, what does this mean? I am going to develop the theory. Based on this novel as an example, I tell you that what happens in love is a very curious thing. The seducer loves several women a little. But some of them get totally hooked on him, in this case the hooked ones are Fortunata and Jacinta, both of them, but to a much greater extent Fortunata who does not have him and who sees him sporadically and suffers his absences for a long time, Jacinta suffers his infidelities, she also suffers, but less than Fortunata. Well, the fact is that we could say that both suffer more than he does.

If we imagine that love is arrows, we could say that an arrow goes from Fortunata to Juan but he does not return the arrow to the other side. Fortunata, not receiving Juan's arrow, is plunged into anguish and despair, and she is a beautiful woman. Fortunata's heart belongs to this man, so although she is free in appearance, she is not free in her feelings. A man, Maximiliano, appears and falls in love with her and she, out of necessity and because it is convenient for her to survive and not be in the fucking street, accepts him, without liking or wanting him. Then Maximiliano shoots an arrow at Fortunata, but she does not return it, because Fortunata's date goes to Juan. Thus Juan not only creates an unfortunate Fortunata, but the man who goes after her, the husband, also suffers because Fortunata does not love him.

However, in the case of Jacinta, she shoots an arrow at him and he returns it a little and this woman suffers less and looks better, although not completely. This woman also had a suitor who did not even dare to declare himself, but he would have been rejected as well. The conclusion of all this is that the cold and hard man comes out well and all the others suffer in cascade. Fortunata suffers for him and Maximiliano suffers for Fortunata who also does not reciprocate, so the desired man does not cause a corpse of love, a girl who has a hard time, but two, the girl and the girl's lover. For this girl is no longer worth to be with others, or even if she is with others she does not feel really happy, nor does she correspond too much. Two amorous corpses are created, the girl whom he abandons and the man in love with that girl who suffers because she does not correspond to him either.

It is like a race in which no one catches up, first goes to Juan, followed by Fortunata who only sometimes catches up with him a little, but escapes again, behind Fortunata goes to Maximiliano who is never close to her and never will be.

In the end, Fortunata dies because she literally dies for him and Maximiliano goes half crazy and ends up in a mental institution.

This is a realistic novel and I give it my validation that this is how it is in reality, nothing has been invented nor has it been sweetened, this is the way things are in life, a few come out quite unscathed and the vast majority suffers a lot.

Here comes the moral issue.

If we were not the ones who correspond little, the ones who make women suffer in variable measure, if they were not behind us, then we would be the ones who go after them and we would live suffering. So if we have to choose between suffering ourselves or that others suffer, we choose that they suffer knowing that we do wrong, but more wrong we would do being us the sufferers, those who go after a woman who likes another man who does not pay attention to her.

Life is hard, all are relationships that almost always end in pain, so we have to take advantage of the good times we have and try to have fun and have a good time, without suffering or making suffer too much, because if we sin of excessive bastards we will fuck people's lives, good women who will suffer excessively for us and this will affect other good men who are after them, and it will be a **chain of pain.**

We don't want that, that's why the sex-terminating angel tries to be fair.

We have an enormous responsibility, that is why we have to be frank and say what our real intention is, so at least we will not deceive good women. They will still fall in love, but less. We will not suffer but we will not make anyone suffer too much either, so we will try to behave in a balanced way. We will only apply dark seduction to very bad women. We are angels of light who use darkness for strict defense.

In the TV series when I saw the actor who played Juan Cruz I said as soon as I saw him, "That's not Spanish! In Spain there are no men like that. I looked on the internet and he was indeed French. The French have fine gestures and an elegant bearing. I immediately associated him with my friend the Frenchman. At the time of the novel there was no man like that in Spain, 1.85 m tall, with such a plant and elegance, I was not mistaken.

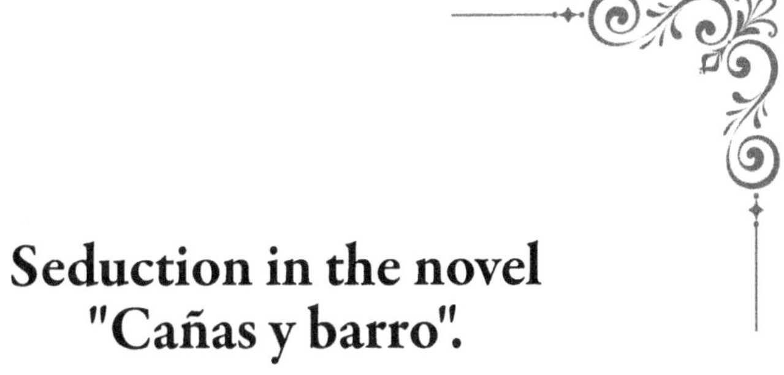

Seduction in the novel
"Cañas y barro".

In this novel by Blasco Ibáñez a fantastic character appears who represents the seducer perfectly, his name is Tonet.

This man was the handsome guy of the town called El Palmar where the novel takes place, this town is very close to Valencia in the middle of the lagoon. Tonet had the women crazy about him, because he was a slim, handsome, handsome guy, with an eternal captivating smile. As soon as I saw him I knew perfectly well that the actor who played him was either a real seducer or a guy with an enormous talent for seduction. This man instead of working with his grandfather fishing in the lagoon, or collecting rice with his father was dedicated to be in the tavern with his faithful friend, forgive me for not remembering the name of this other character ha, ha, ha, ha. They spent all day drinking wine, sometimes they went hunting, or spent the day doing nothing. In short, Tonet was a real bum, so lazy that even his father said he was the shame of the family because he did not want to study or work.

This man had everyone crazy, but especially one already as a child, a girl named Neleta.

This was his girlfriend even though she had to put up with his constant dalliances with all the others. She turned a blind eye because she knew that in the end she was going to be the one. This man went to Cuba to escape the embarrassment of his father, who reproached him for being drunk in the tavern and humiliated him in front of all his followers. Instead of getting back on track, he left. While he was there in Cuba, the war broke out, but instead of being scared or intimidated, he had a great time. In his own letters he wrote to his grieving family, his father, grandfather and sister, he told them that the Guajiras of Cuba were very kind and that they gave him everything he wanted, and when you are a man, they already know what a man wants. This was heard by Neleta herself, who distanced herself from him because of this.

The war lasted a long time and it was not known if he was alive or dead, so between the rudeness he made to Neleta, the lack of concern he showed in his letters for her and not knowing if he was really alive: Neleta made a life for herself and married the richest man in town, a man who had recently been widowed. This husband was a very old man, in fact he was close to death due to poor health.

When they thought he was dead, our man came back, handsome and elegant, as if he were the king himself. All the women in the village were amazed, he came more handsome than ever, with a moustache, white Cuban-style clothes, a white suit and a very elegant hat. Neleta literally dropped her panties and immediately began to cheat on her husband with Tonet.

The story ends like this: when her husband died, Neleta returned to Tonet and soon had a son with him. This son would bring problems because if the people knew about it, they would take away half of the inheritance, and she herself, who became very bad, disowned him. She sent Tonet to abandon him in the incluse, which was an institution for orphaned and unwanted children. What happened was a real drama, because these novels of the nineteenth and early twentieth centuries belonged to realism, and what they were looking for was that, the drama at the end. So the author decided to end the novel in total drama. Our seducer meets a fisherman and kills his own son unintentionally, afraid that he might be seen. He put him under the water of the lagoon so that he would not cry. Then, horrified, he commits suicide.

A very unlikely and not at all logical ending that seeks to transmit, to be like Tonet brings misfortune. This ending is made this way by the tastes of the time, because that was what they wanted to hear. None of that would happen in reality and our man would end up triumphant. In those days when everyone worked and suffered a lot, being so graceful and not very hard-working had to be punished so that society would see him well, hence this tragic ending. He sold more books and pleased the well-to-do people of the time, who did not tolerate that a lazy bum and womanizer ended up well.

What struck me most was that when he arrived, everyone was in a state of grief, afraid to tell him that his bride had married, but he already knew, and with a smile on his face he went there so calmly without jealousy or fear. He went to make friends with the husband and to collect the piece that was really his. This absence of jealousy, worry and infatuation blew my mind, he was a true master in the year 1900.

The history of this work shows that also in Valencia around 1900 there had to be seducers. Blasco Ibáñez was inspired by them to create this character of Tonet, because as I said before, nothing is created out of nothing, everything comes from the observation of real people. There were always cold, hard, carefree, funny and partying seducers. They were not always well regarded, rather almost never, so in the novel he does great mischief in order to please the bemused and formal public. These people hated them, because they felt so inferior that they wished them dead. The writers, knowing all this, put the seducers in their novels committing misdeeds that they would never do, this they would do to please the general public. You and I know that it is one thing to be seductive and another thing to be evil. Seducers are better than the vast majority of people. Seducers love, the envious hate for not being able to be like them. Fucking envy.

This is how they wanted to associate seduction with evil. This novel was written to please the envious and mediocre, which is what abounded, yet the author shows that he is either a seducer himself, or he knows them to perfection. With this lamentable ending, he pleases the masses and at the same time gives himself the pleasure of telling a story where the seducer triumphs in everything during the whole novel except at the end. He sneaks in a story of seduction without them knowing it.

The real end would have been the total triumph of Tonet. But that could not be assimilated in 1900, he had to be crucified, so it was done and everyone was happy. The author tells the great life of this man and the readers are happy that he dies and think, he deserved it for not working, for enjoying so much. Everybody is happy.

Great work.

The Great Reset.

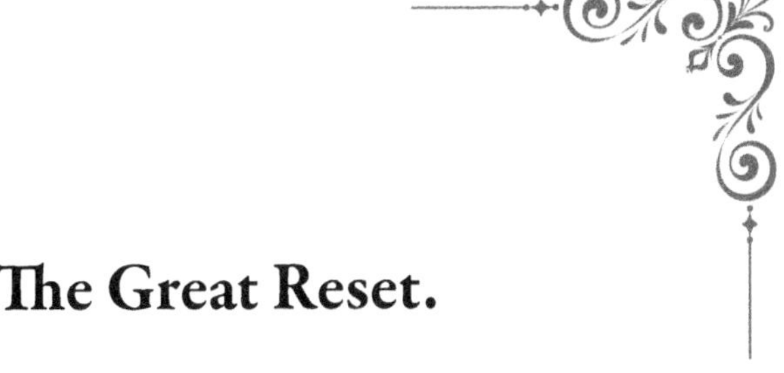

That's why when you have already reached the maximum level, the most important thing is to level down quickly because you are at a level of low competitiveness. Downgrading to Sexductor forces you to be in the fight. That is to say, you are aware that you should be a sex-terminator angel but you prefer to be a simple sexducer and so you reset your account to zero and make your massacre again.

As long as there are goals to strive for, there is life, you can't be in that heavenly state for more than a few months. You must always return to the excitement, stop believing it and return to the game with the illusion of a beginner.

You can't stop this no matter how old you get, it's in your blood. Many are born womanizers by pure genetics and die at 96 years old being womanizers.

Now I only carry one seduced woman. That's today, we'll see tomorrow!

Have a good time.

Having a good time is the great occupation of the sex-terminator angel and of any seducer. If you are happy you transmit that joy to the girls you interact with, your joy attracts them because people like to be with people who bring good feelings. Your function is to always be happy, to be cheerful. They will value this very positively, because people are often sad and they need a dose of good humor.

Girls like to laugh and have a good time. Men are usually quite nervous when interacting with women and this prevents them from flowing well and feeling comfortable with them, so they are neither fun, nor do they have a good time because of that, the tension, knowing that you are playing with getting that hot girl. They are also afraid of saying something unpleasant or of putting their foot in their mouth by giving their opinion on something, and that this is not to her liking. With these limitations they carry out a very politically correct conversation, without risk, but without personal power. This interaction goes through very conventional channels, the interaction is not natural or charismatic.

These men are self-conscious, so the natural charisma that they have to a greater or lesser extent does not flow. The charisma that emanates when you are relaxed and uninhibited. They perceive this, the self-consciousness, the tension and this makes them uncomfortable.

They are uncomfortable because of nervousness and tension, they are self-conscious and do not say very funny things. This causes a slightly tense situation that is not pleasant for them. To compensate for this nervousness these guys put the focus exclusively on them, taking an excessive interest without emanating any charisma and they screw up even more.

You have to be carefree as if you are not playing anything, as if you have known her all your life, cheerful and uninhibited, creating confidence and comfort. By being comfortable you make her feel comfortable. You will have much to gain if, apart from this comfort, you behave in such a way that you are able to generate humor. This way the girl not only does not feel uncomfortable, but has a great time. If we add to all this self-confidence, feeling attractive and emanating that attractiveness through our body language, then the chances of flirting with her will increase exponentially.

It's a matter of making the girl feel good and having a good time. Couple the attraction with the comfort generated and humor and you have a major status on her head.

Be uninhibited, be yourself, be comfortable and calm, as if there was nothing at stake, flow, enjoy yourself, create good feeling and attraction and everything will go smoothly.

Of all the qualities of the JD method I believe that the uninhibited one is the most important, because it is the one that allows you to bring out your true self, the one that shows your charisma and personality. If we are ourselves, even if we enhance who we are, we will be liked or in some cases we will generate rejection, but we will be authentic. Normally, although on the outside they may disagree with what we say, our confidence and charisma generate enough attraction to polish these drawbacks and despite them bring it to us, they love confident and charismatic people.

We will never seduce by saying politically correct things or being neutral, we have to emanate our charisma. Some will not like it, well no one likes everyone, but we will be honest, genuine and authentic. That is why you should never be afraid to give an opinion on something, make sure it is not something excessively controversial, but give your opinion.

Don't be afraid, as Nicolas Cage said in "The Phantom Biker" - You can't live in fear.

Exercise.

The next time you meet an unknown girl, make it your goal to be totally fluid and uninhibited, to be yourself, to be authentic, remind yourself that the only thing you have to do in that interaction is to please yourself and enjoy yourself. Don't be looking out for her and her needs, be looking out for your own enjoyment. Enjoy yourself and she will enjoy herself.

Production.

Seduction is like a business, we must be aware of a very important parameter.

The most important parameter is **production**. What is production? Production is to be flirting as constantly as possible. Girls who go from being without you to being with you, being active, and so being with you they can enjoy the benefits you give them. Production is to go out and pick up girls constantly and effectively pick up girls. You must pick up a lot of girls at the highest rate you can almost all the time. This will produce entries in your production chain. Some may also enter the **circle of trust**. The entries of girls to the circle of power or confidence are the most important objective, because they are girls that you like to be with them, for that reason you fidelize them and you enjoy them more time.

The production will decisively mark the rhythm of entries in this circle. You can make a lot of production but then it may happen that few are worthy of entering this circle of trust. In that case you will have to make a higher production, because few of the girls you pick up are worthy of this. Here there is a flaw and it is that you are picking up girls that you do not really like at all, which is quite difficult but it could happen, then the thing does not progress and they do not enter this circle. This is something quite normal in people who are just starting out and they pick up anyone without having a good connection and without really liking the girl at all, they just pick up for the sake of picking up. A much better way to get girls into the circle is to get them more solidly and make them want to persevere and stay with you. That way with less production you will get a better ratio of girls entering the circle to girls entering the production chain.

If the majority of the girls that you pick up enter the circle of trust, then we will have logistical problems. In this circle of power the girls stay for some time, a very variable time depending on whether we like them more or less, or they give us more or less problems. But they cannot stay there indefinitely. So yes, if girls are entering the circle due to the high volume of production and or our fucking attractive power that retains them, they must also leave at a rate commensurate with the entries. If they are in this circle too much and don't come out, too many accumulate and this will cause problems to be able to see and keep everyone happy. Then you must learn another function, which is to **manage the outputs**.

As I said many times it is of much more master to eliminate than to acquire, eliminate all those that give problems or if they do not give them, those that are less satisfactory, these must leave to be able to give entrance to others that potentially can be better. Sometimes you make a mistake and eliminate girls that were better than others that enter, this you have to go fine tuning it well.

If they accumulate in excess in your circle of trust then you will have serious problems. You will have to sacrifice, the seducer's life is sacrifice and sometimes in cases of high production and power you cannot attend well to all of them and you will have to sacrifice valid girls. This is very hard because they do not deserve it but they must sacrifice even if they are good, because you have a capacity limit and if you reach it you have to sacrifice because you cannot attend them. It is different to eliminate, which is something natural, than to sacrifice.

Then clarifying the vocabulary of the seducer we have the following words.

Acquire. New girl entering our production. She may not make it into the circle of trust, but at least we have acquired her. You should get girls who could potentially enter the circle of trust. A new girl we have picked up can also be called an acquisition.

Within acquisitions there are two types: acquisitions that enter the production chain but do not enter the circle of trust, the so-called **failed acquisitions, or failed entries,** girls who failed once linked. There are also the more successful and solid acquisitions that enter the circle of power.

Eliminate. To remove a girl from our circle of power, and therefore she has already given up, we eliminate her because other better girls appear. This girl is normal, neither good nor bad. It does not cost much pain because we do not have a great attachment to her either. It is a natural part of the productive process.

Sacrifice. To sacrifice is to throw out of our circle a good girl who deserved to be there but because of the attention you have to devote to other even better ones, you can't take good care of her and you have to leave her. She entered the circle of trust and at least we have taken advantage of her a little.

Untapped. Sometimes you have to sacrifice even without having taken advantage of almost nothing and without having come to belong to this circle of trust, and that is very, very, hard, because a valid girl is wasted. It usually happens in times of immense production and when there are many high quality women within the circle, who cannot be left unattended. I will call this **wastage.**

Discarding. To discard is not to pick up a girl that we could pick up, but we don't do it because we foresee the enormous problems that she is going to give us in the future.

I know you spoke here as if they were commodities, it's not my intention to degrade them or anything, it's a way of explaining how production works. I know they have feelings, but you also have feelings and you also suffer, and you feel emotions and feelings with everything you are doing. So even though I'm talking logistically here, all of this involves emotions and feelings that the sex-terminating angel tries to make sure are always beneficial to everyone.

Sometimes there are small pains that are inevitable as all things in life, but I say that the sex-terminating angel seeks to minimize the damage caused.

Inputs, inputs to the comfort circle and outputs. You have to check how the entries are going, how the circle of comfort is going and how the exits are going. The rotation speed of the women in your life, the duration, the good feelings they give you and you give them. There are many things to do and little time to do them and have them all under control.

This is like a factory, the woman arrives a little bored, enters the production line, you make her a transformation, you give her good moments, good sex and good loving emotions, not love, but loving emotions, that make her feel good. And finally when the girl leaves because there are others that you like more, or because you are no longer very excited, she leaves happier than when she entered.

With the production process you have done her a good thing and you have left her with more sexual capabilities, more self-esteem than when she entered, more good memories, you do her a good thing.

Your production is also a mass production on an industrial scale that generates women who are happy to have been with you. That is production, transforming sad women into happy women, after a more or less short or long process, abandoned at the end, but happy.

Some do not make it into the circle of trust where the triad, quartet, quintet, sextet, or whatever is formed, these entries that do not take hold and come and go quickly are failed entries, which did not reach a position and are not really worthy of our attention. **Failed entries or acquisitions**. We'll call these the ones that disappoint and pull out, or the ones that go away on their own because they didn't value us correctly. These girls who were doing well and were in the production chain ended up failing, losing the benefits that this entails, they did not know how to value well. They are eliminated or are eliminated alone.

If a girl rejects us and does not get to be linked, then there is no entry, she is the one who failed. She does not enter the production chain and does not benefit from our services. She failed terribly.

There are in and out, in and out. To summarize.

The inputs in the production chain are the acquisitions... girls who are kissed, or have sex. In the inputs there is a depletion which are the **failed inputs**, girls who disappoint and do not enter the circle of power, these girls quickly become outputs and cease to have the privileges and benefits of being with you.

The exits. They can be two types: quick exits of girls who were unsuccessful entries and did not get to position themselves and exits from the circle of trust or we can also call it **circle of power**, because it gives us power to be with several girls and have the sexual need quite satisfied.

Others are out of the circle of power on their own, in this case they would be **losses**.

Schematically it is like this.

Schematically it is like this.

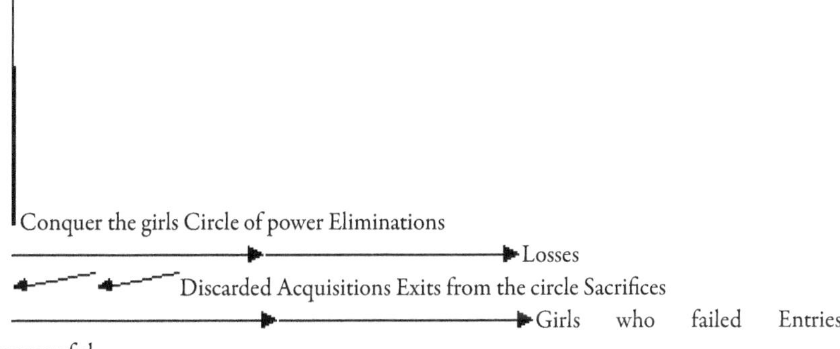

There is no doubt that those who do not reach the circle of power have a much higher turnover than those who enter the circle of power because of their good qualities and stay there for a while.

A seducer has to dedicate himself to his production, so he will increase his fucking power to better conquer the girls. You must also generate a high volume of entries, some are unsuccessful, so these have a very high turnover, with very fast entries and exits. Others enter the circle of power and remain in it as long as we feel like it, until it is impossible to maintain them due to the pressure of new and better entries and the impossibility of attending.

Being a seducer is very hard. You will have to discard some, have a lot of girls that were acquired but disappointed and became quick exits, you must also have the cold blood to eliminate and even more to sacrifice valid girls, who often do not even enter the circle of power and are eliminated without taking advantage of becoming wastes.

You will have to **have the stickiness** to transform the entries (kissed girls), in girls of the circle of power who want to be with us. There is no index to measure how many of those you kiss should enter the power circle, you can kiss many and none of them be valid, or kiss few and all of them be valid, it depends on the connection and understanding you have.

You also have to have a good depth index.

Depth index=Girls had sex/girls kissed=0.5 excellent

0.35 well,

Less than 0.35 bad.

The success rate is = no. of girls you kiss/no. of girls you talk to with the intention of flirting.

You should hit at least one out of ten, rate 0.1, or 10%, being very good if you hit 0.33, that is to say 33% of those you enter.

It's also not about putting all the girls you kiss in the power circle, some of them you already know are going to have a quick turnover and are going to be failed entries that you're eager to eliminate rather than enjoy. Others you can get into the power circle. Generally, wanting to get them into the power circle implies a softness because you want them to last. But there are some magnificent ones that don't give problems and are very well there performing. The ones that know what you look like and sense what you do, but don't care too much.

We can say that there is a slow production which are the girls who enter the circle of power and stay a long time and leave very slowly, and a **fast production** with a lot of rotation that is composed of failed entries that enter and leave quickly, because they do not excite us. Both must be combined. The crazier you are, the more fast production you should do.

Slow production gives knowledge of women and leisurely enjoyment, fast production brings massacres and immense resume and also self-esteem and self-concept of fucker.

Be an artisan who makes a slow, painstaking, beautiful and perfect production, or an industrial-scale producer who barely has time to enjoy his products, due to the very high turnover; in both cases enjoy and be happy.

Release.

You can't feel guilty for being what you are.

Many seducers practice seduction, but then because of all the social pressure that directs you toward formality, they feel a little guilty and think they are doing something wrong, or that they are bad for doing what they do.

You have to free yourself and do what makes you happy, what makes you live, what you enjoy enormously. Of course you do! Why does everyone have to be the same? Why does everyone have to be raising families and taking care of children?

If you have sacrificed that, if you have given that up, you are within your rights to enjoy not only seducing, but also to change girls frequently and live happily. You are doing good too, because you are giving joy, fun, and great sex to those girls who know what they have. They will find themselves a husband when they feel like it, but fortunately it won't be you.

So never feel guilty for being what you are, but rather feel very proud to be doing something that no one dares to do and that everyone is afraid of. If those others believed in themselves as you do, they would do the same and they wouldn't have so many girlfriends and women and they would be doing seduction too. So feel good and even feel superior, because you are superior, because to form a family can be done by anyone who puts the will to formalize, but not everyone can seduce.

Is the wolf sorry when he bites the sheep? Is the tiger sad when he hunts the deer? They are happy and content. You should be aware of your nature and feel proud of being what you are. You are the predator, the hunter who is not satisfied with a monotonous and quiet life. You shun stability, you shun comfort and you love action and self-improvement.

You are the seducer, always be super proud of it.

I am John Danen, the sexducer, the former angel sex-terminator.

With a voice of thunder these words will resound in the air.

Throughout the decades you make your production, sometimes en masse, sometimes little by little with bottlenecks and difficult moments. The production always continues, it is always renewed, because this is not something you can choose or reject, they choose it for you because of your good qualities. You cannot refuse a beautiful woman who opens her legs for you. You are condemned and you really must abide by what they want. A delicious condemnation. You encourage seduction but they really want what you offer.

They all offer themselves, the difference between a sex driver and a regular guy is that the sex driver tries and achieves a lot, while the regular guy gets frustrated, as he doesn't get fucking shit.

This is something that you programmed so much, that it is part of you, it is part of your life, and you cannot leave it in any way. So the years go by, increasing more and more your wisdom. At some point some girl catches you a little bit, but you keep your production at moderate rates. You always know that you can do a lot more and in fact you spend many years swimming between two waters, between going with a more formal girl and continuing to flirt around. That's why you don't make an even more monstrous production, but you still make a huge production. Not at the speed of when you are totally free, but at a good speed.

Little by little the market is becoming more restricted and there are fewer suitable women close to your age, this makes you make even less effort, because there are few prizes to be won, but some remain and as you can't stop, you go on and on. Then comes a time when you do not worry too much about mass production, but rather to enjoy, to be well, to live without trying too hard, and if you produce little, you do not martyr yourself for it. But this is not really something that satisfies, it is simply bearable. Where you are really at ease is in mass production.

On the days when you free yourself from your ties, you release all the accumulated rage and make a small, very concentrated massacre. Sometimes a whole year's production comes out in just one month of true madness. The angel sex-terminator could get a lot more, but he thinks that the efforts he has to make do not compensate for the little booty he can get. A booty of older, heavier and more demanding women.

That's why, because he is above good and evil, the sex-terminating angel gets tired of being an angel. **There comes a day when your blood boils** and you go back to being you, your true self without limits. You stop being a sex-terminating angel and become again a free sex-producer who does his mass production as far as his physique and age allow him. You make an excellent production infinitely superior to all those of your age, you know more than ever and you make real massacres well past 50 and 60.

So it goes in cycles, cycles of higher tranquility and cycles of high production. Life is long and in the end on the day of your death you will have made a brutal production. That's the day your career as a fucker ends.

Decades go by and you go back to places you picked up 20 or 30 years ago, sometimes even going back 40 years, and you think, where are those women I picked up here?

Sometimes by chance you notice a woman and you notice something special about her, because she has something that attracts you to her. It has happened to me to meet women I don't even recognize, but I notice them for something, and then thinking about it I realize that they were women I slept with decades ago. They have something special about them that makes you remember what they were like when you were with them. Quite a few of them are in bad shape, but most of them are fucking great, they are proportionally more attractive than when they were young.

The fucker's life is long and his production is enormous. And so happy and carefree, with times when you go wild and become a real predator who seduces en masse as if you were 23 years old, and others in which you are calmer, life goes by and you make your legend. This will remain in the memory, the production you did, the moments lived, the pleasures felt, this nobody will take it away from you and not even death will be able to erase it, because they will be saved forever in some mystical way in some place of data storage. In my case it will not be necessary, because they will remain in the books that will inspire others to follow my path.

I am not the one who flirts the most, nor the one who fucks the most, nor the one who flirts the easiest, I am not the most in anything, sadly I am not the most dedicated either. All I am is someone who really cares about seducing women and this motivates me and gives me immense satisfaction. I live for this. That's all I really do, live for this.

My production continued, a production that this year makes the number 40, four whole decades, dedicated since 1983. It seems like a company founded in 1983, and you think, wow, it's got a lot of history. Ha, ha. Shortly after I was born, at the age of 13, I started my production. Two centuries of production, man not so much! but a production spread over two centuries, that's true. And so, like a vampire who likes to go out at night, I continue my task, bringing joy, bringing happiness, dust to dust, kiss to kiss, massacre to massacre, increasing the legend.

I'm John "fucking" Danen, a Sexducer, a servant of them. A true feminist, what greater feminist than a man who makes love to women? I am dedicated to the only thing that matters to me, production. I will be immortal through books. And you will know that I existed, you will receive the influence of my words and you will also become a sexducer, a vampire, an artisan producer who pampers his work and at the same time is capable of mass production.

As the Frenchman and I said decades ago

"Here we are and we will never stop."

Who the fuck wants to be formal when you can live a great life seducing women?

I have written a lot about this, but I really have **no words** to describe the immense satisfaction you get when you are seducing, when you go from woman to woman, from bed to bed, when they adore you, when you are the best. You have to live it. All the efforts and sacrifices you make will be returned to you with enormous generosity. You will reach moments of ecstasy of power, of feeling the master, the fucking master, of envying yourself and of liking so much to be you, that you will really love yourself totally.

And no, it doesn't end badly as the envious would like, you will have really lived.

A single day of a sex driver at the peak of his power is worth more than the lifetime of a formal man.

Hypergamy.

Hypergamy is the characteristic possessed by almost all women that induces them to become attached to men of higher social standing than themselves.

Having confidence in yourself is the most important thing and if you do not have it you will be totally excluded from the game, but apart from confidence this is a very important factor, because even if you have great confidence you can be excluded if you are not in the same social status.

I have always been working hard, trying hard to pick up girls, I have never cared about their social class, I just looked for them to look good; I didn't care if they were house cleaners, or marquises.

Marquesas I haven't picked up so I'd better get rid of that. Well, while I was struggling and the girls were not coming to me easily, I observed that other men just being there without doing anything and without being more handsome, more attractive, or having any advantage, were getting better girls than me, also without making much effort.

I decoded this and realized it was due to the social status of these men.

A guy with money has huge advantages, but huge. Let's analyze all the advantages he has.

You can go to better places, like more expensive pubs, you can order better drinks that leave less of a hangover, that are better and that give you a better point. You can travel more, you can travel to more expensive places, stay in better hotels, eat in better restaurants. You will also travel faster or more comfortably, or both, in first class or in a luxurious

Mercedes. It will all be comforts and privileges, albeit at the cost of wasting an enormous amount of money. This comfortable and beautiful life is what they want and they choose these rich people not for what they are, but for what they can make them live. Maybe they are not going to give them such crazy and fun emotions as the sex driver, but they are going to give them very expensive kisses, in places like Rome, Paris, New York, Bali, Tahiti, Bora Bora, Istanbul.

The rich can also wear better and more expensive clothes that are supposed to have more quality. It is a fallacy that they have more quality, what they have is the distinctive mark that separates them from the rest, the logo of the company that manufactures that garment that is a real scam, and neither has more quality, nor is it better than others; but it has the image, the image of that logo that is what differentiates the rich from the poor.

The poor man may be dressed more comfortably and with higher quality, but he will not enjoy the logo of wealth that the brand carries.

The rich will be able to drive a better, more expensive, newer, more technological car. He will be able to travel almost continuously, because many rich people do not even have to work, this is another enormous advantage, because they have money and also time. Their employees already work for them. So they have a lot of leisure some of them and they can always be around for leisure and partying.

Girls see this and notice it and automatically by his clothes and by the demeanor and gestures of a fine person who has not worked too much, a person who has perfected and focused more on elegance and finesse, is immediately detected. He is detected and highly valued by women.

They also have sex advantage that they can have operations that improve their physique, they can have their noses and tummies fixed, they go to gyms, they have personal trainers, dieticians, in short!

I think one of the things that most distinguishes them is that they can go to exclusive, ultra-expensive places, places that only the rich can afford. They can easily find these men there. They drink €300 or €1000 bottles of champagne so happily.

They think that these men can give them a comfortable life of luxury without working in their fucking life. In terms of beauty, the rich man is undoubtedly preferable for these women, and even if he is much uglier, he may be preferable because of the life of luxury he can offer them.

The fucker from Valencia and the Frenchman himself have money, women see that and it also gives them a huge advantage over the rest.

There is also a group of women who are completely inaccessible to any seducer. To this seducer they will only recognize his attractiveness and beauty, they will say that he is phenomenal and that he is a very attractive man; but they will never go with him because of his lack of money, which is what they value most.

In my job I had a very elitist boss, so to speak, who hobnobbed with women of this style, interested in millionaires and in working the bare minimum. Her way to rise in society was to marry them to tie up all their assets. To live the life of luxury that they themselves could not obtain. One of my boss's friends was a particularly beautiful and attractive girl who was very hot; on top of that she was very nice, she was a practically perfect woman, tall, beautiful, nice, everything I said before. This woman who recognized my attributes and my capacity of seduction was never interested in anything amorous with me, but she dedicated herself to go out with millionaires who had expensive Porsches, big companies, or directly with people of the nobility. Finally she ended up married to a count, or duke, I don't remember. That yes, of immense properties and a super comfortable life of multimillionaire. One day I said to this woman, since she didn't pay enough attention to me, why didn't she introduce me to one of her friends, and she said to me, "You look great John, but **you lack a wallet**. They don't want to go with guys like you.

This is hypergamy at its crudest, the only way to seduce these women is to have money and make generous use of it.

The best women, the most beautiful, the most attractive, almost always go with millionaires and they only look at that, the wealth, being annoyed that a good man is going to take them out of their mental schemes and that they can feel attracted by him being poor. This makes them very angry, and very soon if they have had an affair with him, they eliminate him and go back to their millionaire. That is if he manages to pick them up.

Yes, being a millionaire is an advantage, if on top of that you are a millionaire and handsome, then it is an infinite advantage that produces a very high power.

If you are a handsome and seductive millionaire, you will set world records in seduction and flirting will be for you like ordering a beer, a thing of no difficulty. No interested woman in her right mind will be able to resist.

What can the sex producer do in the face of this scenario? The most sensible thing to do is to give up all these women and focus on women of similar quality, but uninterested in material things. The others will never forgive the fact that you are not rich. Love does not exist for them, nor attraction, and if one day they get involved with a poor handsome guy like a model or something like that, they soon leave him in shame, and go back to their rich daddy who gives them luxuries and riches.

It is very difficult to pretend to be a millionaire, if you keep a strong front such as clothing, you will not have money for the other fronts which are travel, hotels, meals, cars, houses, in short, you will be found out!

In the face of this, either you give them up, or you get really rich, or you don't give a fuck about all this bullshit and focus on your good women who do value you for yourself and not for your possessions.

Then they say that women are good and praiseworthy, well this does not happen with men except on very rare occasions, and on top of that it is frowned upon that there are men interested in taking money from women. However it is super well seen that they do it, more outdated machismo.

In short, don't give a shit because you are only missing out on bad, superficial, interested women, who don't love you, and who are not worth meeting or flirting with, because in addition to all the money they will take from you, they will only give you annoyances and a false love, that as soon as you don't pay for their whims will disappear completely. They are paid girlfriends. There is love if there is money.

The phoenix.

The sex producer always resurfaces, like everyone else you have bad times and you can have quite big crises, but you are the sex producer and you are aware of being one, so you always come back triumphant to the market. It is all a mental issue, you can have a crisis at eighteen, at 25, at 30, at 40, at 60 and maybe your best moment will be at 75. It only depends on your mind, on your security and confidence. It is not being or not being anything, it is how you feel about yourself. **As soon as you like yourself, they start to like you.**

So at eighteen I was booming and at nineteen I was retired with a girlfriend, at 22 I resurfaced and at 25 I sank again, at 26 I resurfaced again and I was going strong until I was 44. There was another crisis and I resurfaced again, there was another one around 52 and I resurfaced again.

Nothing and nobody can stop your power, as soon as you restore your head, you become aware of your fucking power, and you feel attractive again, you dedicate yourself much more, you become motivated again, and you are back to sweep the market.

Hermes Gasparini.

I am a fan of arm wrestling and follow quite a few characters like Devon Larrat or John Brzenk. Now there has appeared a new one named Hermes Gasparini who is currently ranked number two in the world and is only beaten by Levan Saginashvili.

This man Levan is a real monster, a giant with monstrous arms and body and weighs almost 200 kilos. He is big but he looks like a very good man, there is no one who can beat him. Hermes Gasparini takes him on and puts him in trouble and he is one of the few in the world who can do it.

Well, we are like this man Gasparini, a man of almost normal appearance, he looks very strong, but he is not a monster, he is even an attractive guy, a normal guy who has become muscular, a guy who can flirt perfectly, a guy who looks almost like a normal man but who is able to stand up to the number one in the world and who usually beats all the others.

We are like this man, for we are not the tallest, not the best looking, not the strongest, not the smartest, not the most attractive, not the most confident, not the most fun. We are not the best at anything, but we have a combination of qualities that make us super competitive, and without being the best at anything, not even at the dedication that this game requires, we beat practically everyone; that is being a sex driver. A man with a normal appearance, strong in all fields, but who is not the best in any of them and who beats everyone almost every time. Seducers do more with less, we go much, much higher than you can imagine.

We apply a force to seduction that can be compared to a hydraulic press. A force that never ceases. An ever-increasing force that totally crushes the resistance of the girls.

Tricked game.

Many times girls interact with us, but they do it not because they are attracted to us, but because of some hidden interest. This interest can often be to get some benefit, such as an invitation to a drink or beer. Most of the time they do it to show off and make others jealous who are the object of their interest. I have called this "trick play".

As soon as you detect the tricky game, do not allow him to continue doing it, tell him that you know what he is doing, that he is using you, that you are not stupid and that you are aware of his tricks. Make yourself respected and do not follow his trick game. Do not say anything to her about hooking up with her, nor try to pick her up. Don't give her that pleasure. They have everything they want when they want, they even have enough, let's not boost their ego any more, identify their trick game and stop it at the root.

You will know if there is a trick game when she is with you but is constantly looking towards someone else, or if she keeps a cold and distant attitude, more concerned about being seen with an attractive guy like you, than what you are telling, or what is going on between the two of you. These are feminine wiles that of course we should not tolerate.

Be cheerful and fun.

Partying should be your religion. Take advantage of any occasion to go out, even days when there is not much atmosphere are appropriate to have a good time, because it is easier to establish contact. The party is life.

We have to totally banish apathy, boredom or monotony from our personality. We have to be true fans of the party and take our own party everywhere we go. Wherever we go we leave our mark, we can go singing in the street, whistling, greeting people we don't know, showing the world that we are happy and everything is going great.

The natural state of the sex driver is euphoria. Euphoria because you have the life you want to have, because you do what you like, because you enjoy immensely what you do, because you have huge benefits derived from this lifestyle, such as beautiful girls you kiss, beautiful girls you sleep with, joys, kisses, affection, etc. What you like most about your life is the joy, the joy of being this way, the joy of having a good time going out and partying more often than you should.

They detect this joy and they love it, because people's lives are quite boring and monotonous. If you make them laugh, bring them joy and they have a great time with you, you tell them funny stories, you are uninhibited and fun, they will want to be with you, because everyone likes to have a good time. Friends who are enthusiastic about your overwhelming personality will also want to come with you. Play music, listen to it loud and live every day like it's a fucking party. Let others be worried and overwhelmed, that's not for you, always optimistic, always active, always with new exciting projects. You bring your contribution which is joy and fun. Joy and fun are your religion and you practice them constantly.

No fears, no insecurities, no what people will say! You do what you want when you want, you laugh out loud, you whistle, you sing and dance in the street, you enjoy your party, nothing can take away your party, your party is in your mind.

The last men seducing at the end of days, once again.

Yes, there was a sex-terminating angel who is no longer a sex-terminator and becomes a sex-ducer. Here and now I am writing this book for you, I was an angel who lived infinite adventures, decoded women in every way, and did everything imaginable. All of it I wrote in all the books.

It's all been said, it's all been written, it's all done.

All you have to do is read each and every one of the above books and train yourself to be that excellent version of yourself to take the market by storm. After that, enjoy the wonder of being a sex driver who picks up more girls than he can handle.

Little by little you will go up the ladder and reach the top, fall down and get back up again, and rise again and get over your head with so many successes, and so on and so on indefinitely.

In the end, if you have really renounced to a greater or lesser extent to conventionalisms, you will live a great life enjoying girls throughout your life. If you want, you can get a girlfriend whenever you want, do whatever you want, always going back to the market to enjoy your enormous capabilities.

As a former sex-terminator angel I say don't want to be a sex-terminator angel, be in the game and totally enjoy it.

The best adventures are yet to come.

The best women are yet to come.

The greatest power is yet to be achieved.

We are always under construction and our work is never finished, but we are almost always competitive except in times of crisis and breaks from the hustle and bustle.

Our natural environment is the pub and the discotheque, where flirting takes place.

We are the last men seducing at the end of days, and after the end of days passing pandemics and bullshit, the last men are still seducing after the end of days as survivors of everything.

Here we are and we will never stop.

Stay tuned as my next book "The Detector" will give you the keys to visually interpret their body language.

All has been said, all has been written, all is done. Ha, ha, ha, ha it's never all said and done, the production must go on, Show must go on.

I will continue to make books as long as I see something I can improve on everything told. The production in this field has been monstrous and now I'm going to spend some time doing what I love most, the real production, the real me. It's been three years of writing a lot, time to play, time to, time to...

Seduce the pretty girls!

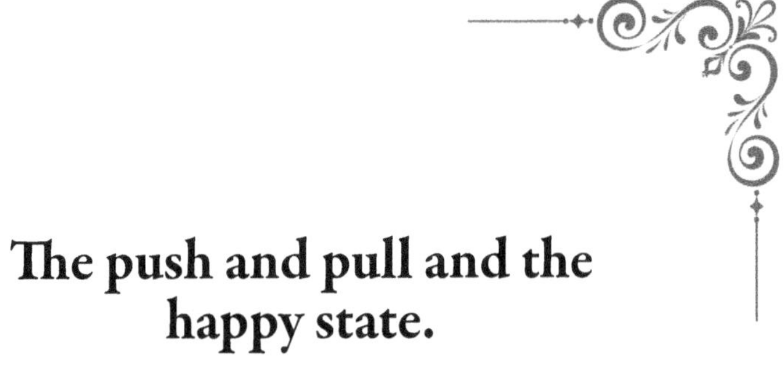

The push and pull and the happy state.

Perhaps one of the most important things in all of seduction is your inner state of mind. When you feel enthusiastic, confident and secure, when you are eager to make contact with girls, when you don't shy away from them, when you encourage interaction, when you enjoy getting into them, this is a great sign that you are in an optimal state to seduce them. You are carefree, uninhibited, and fun the three most powerful dis, you accompany with a little comfort and complicity, you are making little jokes, playing with them, using the tug of war, showing a very clear interest and then withdrawing it by saying it was all a joke, making them feel emotions and then denying them, in that fun state, carefree of everything, in which you fool around with them, but then say it's all a lie and you are really fooling around with them; you show that you have all the weapons to seduce and they like it. Okay this is fine if you do this pull and push in an occasional and moderate way. That's masterful.

You keep playing by messing with them, making more jokes, throwing hints at them, being cheeky by mixing it all with humor.

That, that you play with them, that you show a sexual love interest and then you take it back, that you baffle them, that you go from the top, from the superiority of the guy who has plenty of women, who plays with a woman because he sees her as a little girl, as someone who has some good qualities but who is not of interest to him, so you drive them crazy. As I said before, everything in moderation.

You can only do this push and pull if you are a jerk when you don't like anything and you don't care about a girl and so you torture her a little bit. However you should do it when you really like her in light mode. Sometimes someone overdoes the jokes and it's a bit tiresome and heavy, but if you do it just enough it will be effective.

Important.

I don't like to abuse this method of push and pull, because it seems to me that you lower them and even humiliate them a little with so many jokes and so much superiority. I often find the person who does it arrogant and unpleasant, that's why I don't use this technique too much, because I find it unpleasant towards them and excessively devaluing. It is necessary to do it in a small measure sometimes, not to be all the fucking time undervaluing them. To me, the one who practices it seems to me to be very interested in it, wanting to appear indifferent and I don't like him at all.

They are not very much valued, but to be all the fucking time playing, making jokes, undervaluing them without stopping, seems to me to be of imbeciles. Assholes who are tiresome, unpleasant and assholes. These practitioners go around bragging about their cockiness and what they transmit to me is just the opposite, I see them as slimy, starving, dependent and super needy. They are always very affected by them, they look very needy because they are always flirting and making insinuations and they are excessively artificial.

They think they are superior, wanting to flirt in front of you, and that is what they want, that you feel shy and silly next to them because you don't do all their nonsense, all their scorn and bad jokes to the girls.

Some with low self-esteem flirt, but I don't like them, and I don't like them, because I find it unpleasant to continually belittle them. It is necessary to be amusing sometimes to do a minimum of this in moments of cockiness, but not to abuse.

This method fails because here there is no connection, no comfort, no complicity and if you attract her enough with the pull and push something is missing, something is missing that you really feel connected with her, that you like something about her, and that you value her. Little but something.

The scornful joker is a lout, who is a flirt and apparently flirts, but doesn't go too deep and who really makes people feel bad with so much arrogance and absurd jokes. There is no need to be such a jerk.

Showing interest and then withdrawing it as a joke, playing with them from on high, is fine, but don't be tiresome and base everything on that.

It is enough to be in what I have called "the happy state". This happy state is a state of mind where you are fun, happy and carefree, but you also connect and create a nice bond.

You play with them a little bit sometimes, they are not afraid of you at all. If you play with girls and say funny things to them you will have good power and attract.

Use sometimes in occasions of great connection and complicity with her a little bit of pull and push, without abusing, without being a pimp for an hour and ridiculing her.

I have emphasized too much on hardness and it is very important that you focus on reaching this happy state using the jd method. You need to not only enter them easily, but enjoy entering them very much, fool around with them with push and pull very moderately, make playful advances and then withdraw your interest.

Be in a happy state, use pull and push as little as possible, uninhibit yourself, flow, don't be afraid of them, have fun, take your fucking party inside and transmit it to them live. You have to look more for fun than flirting, having a good time, laughing, making them laugh, create attraction and but don't forget to create the connection between the two of you, she also has to be comfortable and at ease with you. She has to see a little good side of you, feel a connection with you, feel that you care a little about her and that underneath the appearance of a confident guy there is a good person.

The pull and push in its most radical state is used by guys who are arrogant, who think they are better than the rest, that people don't like them, that if they pick up someone it's because they don't have self-esteem and that they are guys who are not really good people, nor do they contribute anything good to seduction. They create attraction but not connection.

A sexductor, even if he is a bastard, even if he is shameless, even if he is naughty and even if he thinks he is better than them, has an inner good part that they also glimpse sometimes and that creates enough connection and enough comfort for them to value you well.

You can be harsh and you can punish very harshly, but I really don't like the funny jokers with their constant put-downs of the girls. The pull and Push as the only weapon of seduction is used by the imbecile of the people, an imbecile who thinks he has done a lot in seduction by picking up six girls and that a real sex producer withdraws from the market very quickly, because the one who was giving so much trouble with his imbecilities to do nothing, the sex producer seduces doing the fourth part of his effort.

The "yes" and the "noes".

I'm going to tell you here how women behave when you propose something to them and in general how to know when the interaction is going towards a yes or a no. Women communicate in a certain way. Women communicate in a very indirect and ambiguous way, they find it difficult to say no, they avoid confrontation; therefore it is very easy to identify when the interaction is going towards no and also when it is going towards yes.

Yes No

Things flow easily. Obstacles to meeting are constantly appearing
The meeting will take place. The meeting does not materialize.
She calls you. You call her.
You get the date the first time. She goes on and on.
She likes what you tell her. She's upset about your hobbies.
She answers messages quickly. Messages go unanswered for days.
Gives you the phone. Gives you other ways to contact her than by phone.
You meet in less than a week. Time goes by and the date never materializes.
He says things and does them. She does not fulfill anything of what she says.
She is willing to travel to meet you. She does not want to travel.
Asks questions about you. She only talks about herself.
She was anxious to meet. The less haste the better.
She has availability. She is always busy.
She never postpones an appointment. She postpones appointments.
You feel like talking to her and are comfortable. She is frustrating to talk to.
She asks you about your old girlfriends. Tells you that she hopes you find love.
She calls you by name She calls you friend.
What she tells you about her past is in little detail. Tells you in detail about her past affairs.
Shows interest in doing things with you. Talks about introducing you to friends of her.
When you make appointments, she is always on time.
She trusts you. She defines herself as distrustful.
She says we. Never says "we".

She says phrases with double sexual intent. She never says things with double sexual intent.
You talk about sexual topics. Sexual topics are absent from the conversation.
She listens to you and is interested. You can tell she doesn't care about you.
You think about her and like her. You think about her and you don't like her.
She laughs at the things you tell her. Bland and dry.
Communicates often If you don't talk to her she doesn't talk to you.
In your presence she approaches you physically. When you are with her she moves away from you.
She touch you She doesn't touch you.
She thinks of you as a nice guy. She brings out physical and personality flaws in you.
Interacting with her makes you feel attractive. You can tell she thinks poorly of you.
Approves of your past. Considers that your past is not normal.
She accepts your proposals. Considers that it is too soon.
Gives you confidence and encourages you to be you. It coaxes you and minimizes you.
Values you. She puts you down.

IN THE "YES" COLUMN the girl has validated you as a man suitable to be with her, and may even have already pre-selected you, giving you favorable treatment over the others. In the "no" column she is always procrastinating, answering ambiguities, stonewalling, saying unkind things, showing little appreciation for you. In this case she has already qualified you as unfit to be with her, but she does not dare to say it openly, so she will have you wearing yourself out, you will try to make something happen, however she will not tell you a blunt no, a no openly, her strategy will consist of postponing and postponing, and making excuses, until you get tired so that you finally throw in the towel and give up.

They are not direct, they find it hard to confront, they prefer this strategy of putting obstacles and excuses.

When you are talking to several women on the internet or in real life, rate them on this scale, and place first in your preferences those who have a higher proportion of "yeses" and last those who have a higher proportion of "noes". Those whose behavior is almost always in the "no" column are not worth insisting on, abandon them, don't try to meet or anything, if they are interested they will talk, but they won't, because that's how they start, that's how they end, and if they had difficulties at the beginning, they will have even more difficulties at the end, so focus only on those who have a high proportion of "yeses". Stick to the easy ones, get rid of the difficult ones and let them put up with it.

Final advice.

The sex-terminating angel is a very crazy state, you have to fight, not settle. If you want to get high in seduction I give you some final tips so you can achieve it.

- Do not be discouraged, this is very hard and you must assume it.
- Be willing to sacrifice everything for seduction.
- Study the JD method and read all my books.
- Learn how to relate to them correctly once you have a relationship.
- Put your heart into it.
- Put enormous dedication and practice.
- Be patient.
- Enjoy everything, the interaction, the learning, the failure and the victory.
- Visualize yourself achieving your successes.
- Be proud to be a man.
- Be proud of doing what you do.
- Once you are bonded, don't soften more than necessary.
- Persevere and overcome everything, crises, girlfriends, failures.
- Be aware that despite being hard, this is the best life in the world.
- Success depends exclusively on you because you can change all your circumstances.
- Take more risks.
- Start today.
- Celebrate your successes.
- Value yourself higher than them.

- Take care of your physique and image.
- Work on your self-concept of who you want to be.
- Follow me on social media.

Let's play!

Don't miss out!

Visit the website below and you can sign up to receive emails whenever John Danen publishes a new book. There's no charge and no obligation.

https://books2read.com/r/B-A-FUKJ-IFBNC

BOOKS 2 READ

Connecting independent readers to independent writers.

Did you love *Sex-Terminating Angel*? Then you should read *Dark Seduction*[1] by John Danen!

[2]

My darkest and most evil book. To be used only in cases that require our strongest defense against abuse. Using dark seduction magically makes them become nice to you.

---

1. https://books2read.com/u/3k25oK

2. https://books2read.com/u/3k25oK

Also by John Danen

Seduction 5.0
S.A.X.
Chicas complicadas
Seducción 5.0
El libro del tonto
Macho Alpha
Macho alpha extracto
La seducción después de la pandemia
Terriblemente atractivo
Seducción 5.1
Sedução 5.1
How to be Cool and Attractive
Sedução. Avançada. X.
Garotas complicadas
¡Basta de ser buen chico! Sé un chico malo.
El método JD. El método de seducción de John Danen
El arte de agradarte a ti mismo
¡Basta ya de abusos! ¡Defiéndete!
Enought with the abuse! Defend yourself!
Máster en seducción
Las mujeres. El amor. Y el sexo.
Supera la dependencia emocional
Atrae mujeres con masculinidad
JD Absoluta seducción
El fracaso del amor

Entender a las mujeres

La vida del seductor sinvergüenza y encantador.

El arte de la dureza

Terrivelmente atraente

Deixe de ser um bom da fita! Seja um mauzão.

Superar a dependência emocional

A arte de se agradar

Pare o abuso! Defenda-se!

O fracasso do amor.

O método JD

Don´t Be a Good Boy! Be a Badass

Complicated girls

The Art of Pleasing Yourself

Duro y Sinvergüenza

Mestre en sedução

JD Method

The Failure of Love. The Trap of Serious Relationships

Master in Seduction

A. S. X. Advanced. Seduction. X

Women. Love. Sex

How to Become a Real Man. Be an Alpha Male

Attract Women with Masculinity

JD Absolut Seduction

Understanding Women

The Life of the Shameless and Charming Seducer.

The Art of Toughness

Tough and Shameless

Überwindung der Emotionalen Abhängigkeit

Maître en séduction

Schrecklich Attraktiv

Surmonter la Dépendance Émotionnelle

L'art de la dureté

Die Kunst der Zähigkeit

Hör auf, ein guter Junge zu sein, sei ein böser Junge
Assez D'être un Bon Garçon ! Sois un Mauvais Garçon.
Die Kunst, sich Selbst zu Gefallen
Dur et sans Vergogne
Hart im Nehmen und Schamlos
L'art de se Plaire à soi-Même
Das Scheitern der Liebe
L'échec de L'amour.
Meister der Verführung
Die JD-Methode
Maestro di Seduzione
Terriblement Attrayant
La Méthode JD
Capire le donne
Compreendendo as Mulheres
Comprendre les Femmes
Die Frauen Verstehen
Les Filles Compliquées
Komplizierte Mädchen
JD Séduction Absolue
La Vie du Séducteur Charmant et sans Vergogne
Les Femmes. L'amour. Et le Sexe.
Mâle Alpha
S.A.X.
V.F.X.
Donne. Amore. E il sesso.
Ragazze Complicate
Superare la Dipendenza Emotiva
Seduzione. Avanzata. X.
Dark Seducción
Il Fallimento Dell'amore.
Il Metodo JD
Alphamännchen

Atrair Mulheres com Masculinidade

Attirare le donne con la Mascolinità

Attirer les Femmes par la Masculinité

Mit Männlichkeit Frauen Anziehen

Frauen. Liebe. Und Sex.

L'arte di Piacere a se Stessi

Mulheres. Amor. E Sexo.

JD Seduzione Assoluta

JD Absolute Verführung

JD Sedução Absoluta

Das Leben des charmanten, schamlosen Verführers

Smettila di Fare il Bravo Ragazzo! Essere un Cattivo Ragazzo.

La Vita del Seduttore Affascinante e Spudorato

A Vida do Sedutor Encantador e sem Vergonha

Macho Alfa

Uomo Alfa

Séduction 5.0

Verführung 5.0

Seduzione 5.0

Duro e Senza Vergogna

Duro e Sem Vergonha

L'arte della Durezza

A Arte da Dureza

The Fool's Book

Das Buch der Dummköpfe

Il Libro dei Pazzi

O Livro do Tolo

Dark Seduction

Dunkle Verführung

Sedução Escura

Dark Seduction

Seduzione Oscura

Le livre du fou

Como materializar lo que deseas con el fxxxxxx power
Como materializar o que você quer com o Fxxxxxx Power
El ángel Sex-terminador
El seductor vampiro
O Vampiro Sedutor
Sex-Terminating Angel
The Vampire Seducer
How to Materialize What You Want With The Fxxxxxx Power
El camino del maestro
Il vampiro seduttore
O camiño do mestre
La via del maestro
Der verführerische Vampir
Le sedusant vampire
Der Weg des Meisters
La voie du maître de la séduction
The Way of the Master
Come materializzare ciò che si desidera con il Fxxxxxx Power
Wie Sie Ihre Wünsche verwirklichen können mit dem Fxxxxxx Power
El método EDP
O método EDP
The EDP method

About the Author

Español.

Soy un hombre vividor y divertido que busca el lado bueno de las cosas siempre.

Mi experiencia es el campo de las relaciones personales y de la seducción. Por eso tras dedicarme larguísimas décadas a ello, quiero trasmitir mis conocimientos. Para que las nuevas generaciones tengan unos conceptos que les den una ventaja competitiva sostenible y poderosa en el campo del amor.

Quiero ayudarte a a conseguir tus metas.

Portugués.

Sou um homem animado, e divertido, que sempre procura o lado bom das coisas.

Minha experiência está no campo das relações pessoais e da sedução. É por isso que, após décadas de dedicação a ela, quero transmitir meus conhecimentos.

Quero ajudá-los a alcançar seus objetivos.

Inglés

I am a lively and fun man, who always looks for the good side of things.

My experience is in the field of personal relationships and seduction. That is why, after decades of dedicating myself to it, I want to pass on my knowledge. So that the new generations have concepts that give them a sustainable and powerful competitive advantage in the field of love.

I want to help you achieve your goals

Français Je suis un homme vif et drôle qui cherche toujours le bon côté des choses.

Mon expérience se situe dans le domaine des relations personnelles et de la séduction. C'est pourquoi, après m'y être consacré pendant des décennies, je veux transmettre mes connaissances. Pour que les nouvelles générations disposent de concepts qui leur donnent un avantage concurrentiel durable et puissant dans le domaine de l'amour.

Je veux vous aider à atteindre vos objectifs.